Alienated Parent Journal

An expressive writing guide for coping with child estrangement

Jonathan Hatch, MA, CPRP.

Publisher's note:

This book is published with good faith efforts to be accurate and informative in the subject matter covered based on the author's education, experience, and personal opinion. This book is for educational purposes and in no way, constitutes the rendering of psychological, legal, or any other professional service. This book is not an appropriate replacement for professional mental or physical health services. If professional help is needed please seek the services a qualified professional.

Published by Father 2 Father, Inc

Copyright © 2017
All rights reserved.
ISBN-13:978-1985099166
ISBN-10:1985099160

Dedication

I dedicate this book my wife who stood by me through the ups and downs, the depression and anger, the bitter victories and crushing defeats of my own alienation with my son. Erin, your support has always been, and continues to be, nothing short of miraculous and I am thankful for it every day.

To my son, I am sorry for the position you were put in. The conflict was not yours to bear and I am so sorry we lost so much time. I have always loved you, I will always love you, nothing can ever change that.

I would also like to dedicate this book to every parent who has been estranged from a child, may your pain ease but never go away completely. This book is for you to process the grief that you dare not speak and the hope you dare not hope. This book is for you to manage your own feelings so that you can be a more effective parent, in whatever role that is, in the face of alienation and estrangement.

About the author

Jonathan Hatch is a psychotherapist practicing in the suburbs of Boston MA and an alienated father.

As a mental health clinician, he has helped many people with a variety of needs including severe cognitive impairments, substance addiction, family dynamics, and mood disorders within a variety of treatment approaches. He believes in cultivating the courage to accept the unacceptable, challenge assumptions, and always seek solutions rather than focusing on problems.

As an alienated father he has felt firsthand the pain and grief of losing a child's love and affection through the dynamics of hostile aggressive parenting and alienation. He has fought the uphill struggle of a non-custodial parent in the family courts system countless times. He has battled with his own self-doubt, frustration, and depression through the years of being estranged from his son.

About Father 2 Father, Inc

Father 2 Father is a 501(c)(3) nonprofit organization founded by the author of this journal and dedicated to helping men become the best fathers they can be. We hope to be a resource for dads who are struggling with the challenges of fatherhood or with the pain of alienation and estrangement. We are a community for all dads to help each other through sharing stories and experience, lending support and forming relationships. We think fatherhood is the best gift in the world and hope to spread this message to combat father absenteeism and the stigma of fathers being "second class parents". We absolutely believe that men can fulfill any aspect of parenting and that an empowered dad, is a great dad! If you have any questions, or would like to get involved with F2F, please contact us through our Facebook page.

www.facebook.com/father2father/

A portion of the proceeds from the sale of this book goes to helping the mission of Father 2 Father, Inc. Thank you for your support!

Contents

Introduction

If you've bought this book chances are you're suffering a pain that many just don't understand. Those who are not alienated or have never been "targeted parents" will not understand or apricate the depths of the frustration, despair, and anguish that results when your child is brainwashed to reject you. As a pathological paradigm, Parental Alienation is poorly understood by mental health clinicians, family court judges and lawyers, teachers, and the general public. Parental Alienation is not a required subject of any educational program for professional competencies of social work, mental health, or law. In fact, the very existence of this phenomena is hotly debated among factions in the "divorce industry".

Let me assure you that Parental Alienation (PA) and Parental Alienation Syndrome (PAS) is real. It is real for the destruction of a healthy and loving parent-child relationship. It is real for the deficits in the child's academic, social, and/or emotional development that can be directly attributed to the high conflict nature of divorce in the US. It is real for the time that is lost that can never be gotten back. It is real for the pain, the grief, the depression, one goes through in face of such unjustified rejection and the loss of their child. Parental alienation is real.

A parent who in the course of a custody dispute, or other split-family conflict, brainwashes their children to reject the other parent is, in my estimation, guilty of child psychological abuse. As parents, our job is to protect our children from all threats. To see that they grow as healthy and happy as possible and become successful productive members of society in whatever vocation that provides them the most satisfaction. A part of this responsibility is to make sure we are strong enough to meet the challenge. In cases of PA and PAS the pain and depression can easily overwhelm personal resiliency and precipitate either an overreaction or an underreaction to the alienating parent's behavior, i.e. the alienating tactics, which will be discussed later.

The purpose of this journaling guidebook is to provide you, the alienated/targeted parent, with some education and tools to keep yourself healthy through the fight to maintain a healthy relationship with your child/children or through the reunification process once the estrangement has been established. This book can also serve to help you cope with the day to day living in the aftermath of an estrangement. This book is divided into 3 parts. Part 1 is information based and reviews the process of coping with emotional distress and trauma through expressive writing. Part 1 also provides a brief overview of PA and PAS, what it is and how to recognize it. Also, this book offers a very brief review of stress management to help you maintain your own strength and resilience through the difficult challenge ahead. Part 2 is the expressive writing assignments. In this section, there are prompts for you to write about specific topics, for a set amount of time along a specific progression. This is where the hard work is. If done correctly, you should be striking the cords of your emotional heartstrings and really connecting with the underlying basis of your distress. Part 3 is reserved for you to use as you will. It is in essence space for free writing where you can revisit and expand on any of the writing assignments or keep it as a place to update after part 2 and use some of the skills you've learned to process future events.

Part 1

How To Use This Book

This book is intended to be an expressive outlet for the processing of complex emotions. It is not meant to be a substitute for or replace the services of a qualified mental health counselor or psychiatrist. This book can be used as an adjunct to treatment and can be incorporated into regular therapy.

Read through part 1, take part 2 step by step, and use part 3 as you will as an ongoing journal. Write as much or as little as you want. This is an open process determined by you. You can create your own writing prompts or none at all. The best use of this journal is to find quiet space free from distractions. You don't have to show it to anybody, not even your therapist. Keep in a secure place so that you will be free to write anything you want.

What is Expressive Writing?

Expressive writing and journaling are similar but not necessarily the same. Where journaling (daily writings of events) may have some therapeutic benefit, expressive writing is specific and targeted to explore the content of emotional distress and trauma. First introduced in the 1960s, and popularized in the 1980s, expressive writing has been shown to help people suffering with many diagnosable disorders such as depression, anxiety, substance abuse, eating disorders, obsession-compulsive disorders, and Post-traumatic stress disorder (PTSD). Expressive writing can also benefit the non-diagnosable but significant problems that impact us a great deal such a low self-esteem, grief and loss, coping with chronic illness, and various interpersonal issues. The practice of expressive writing, although most often considered an adjunct to traditional psychotherapy, is recognized as a therapeutic modality in its own right. In other words, a great number of people who are experiencing emotional or interpersonal challenges in their lives could process and resolve their issues with only pen and paper. However, this is not to say that expressive writing is sufficient treatment in all cases. Rather, the need for expressive writing only or in conjunction with traditional psychotherapy will depend on the circumstances and the individual's severity of symptoms.

Expressive writing as a therapeutic modality, differs markedly from daily journaling. Although the two terms are sometimes used interchangeably, expressive writing aims to probe and process the inner most thoughts and bring about a certain level of insight to what is at the root of the emotional distress. Whereas journaling typically focuses on a descriptive narrative of events. This narrative by its nature can lack emotional depth because of the distance the writer creates when writing chronological events. For instance, if you were to journal about a troubling event such as a fight with a dear friend, you would write about the argument. She said this then I said that… etc. Whereas an expressive writing assignment would prompt you "dig deep" and write about how you felt as a result of the argument in addition to what was said.

How Can Expressive Writing Help Me?

Studies show expressive writing can benefit both mental and physical health. Participants in these studies have shown less venerability to illness by improved immune functioning and decreased visits to health care providers in the months following an expressive writing intervention. There are reports of improved working memory and cognitive functioning as well. This is all in addition to improvements in mental and emotional wellbeing. Overall since the 1980s more than 200 studies have been published that document such benefits. To be clear, expressive writing cannot by itself fix problems and heal the sick. It can, however, help prepare you to meet whatever challenge you face with a clear mind and emotionally centered.

Do I Need A Therapist, Is Writing Enough?

This is a difficult question to answer. The short answer is maybe. Journaling and expressive writing is not a cure-all, and it not a substitute for psychiatric treatment. Seeking treatment would depend on the severity of your symptoms, your daily functioning, and the circumstances your symptoms occur. All this can be assessed by a qualified professional. Or if you prefer, there are a number of online symptom checkers that can assist you in making a decision whether or not to seek out the services of a counselor or a psychologist. You can find these symptom screeners on websites such as Psychology Today and WebMD to name a few. However, it is important to keep in mind that the best sign that a therapist may be helpful is if you think you could benefit from talking to a professional.

What Do Therapists Do, And How Do They Differ From Expressive Writing?

Therapists do not have a magic wand or a crystal ball (I wish they did). They cannot "fix" unpleasant things, that's not what they are there for. They simply listen. They listen to your inner most thought processes and how you interpret the world around you. They offer suggestions towards resolving those issues in the healthiest way possible. There is some of overlap between medical treatment and mental health treatment. Both seek to remediate pathologies, both benefit from proactive strategies, and when indicated, both physical and mental health can benefit greatly from medication. There are significant biological processes at work that contribute to mental health symptoms. However, there is a duality in mental health treatment that incorporates both an art as well as a science. This is evident in the efficacy rates in talk therapy vs medication. Very often, especially with Cognitive-Behavioral Therapy (CBT), talk therapy is as effective or more effective than medication for mental health disorders. The exact cause of mental disorders is still unknown. Therefore, both medical therapies and talk therapies are best guesses. They are evidence based and theory informed, but they are still guesses. We only know the treatments have worked, after they work.

Many people assume that once you meet a doctor or a therapist you have to stick with that provider, this is not so. Finding a good therapist is a bit like car shopping. They are both an important decision, and really when you think about it, an investment. By taking the therapist for a "test drive" you get to know a little about who they are and what kind of therapy they practice. A psychoanalytically oriented therapist may ask you about your childhood and connect those experiences to your unconscious conflicts to bring about some sort of epiphany or insight into maladaptive patterns. Those breakthroughs can be lifechanging. However, other therapist may ascribe to a more person-centered or humanistic philosophy where disclosures of conflicts and troubled emotions are met with unwavering support and reassurance. There is a considerable amount of research supporting the efficacy of such a treatment modality. However, maybe your kind of car (if we're sticking with the car shopping analogy) is as functional as it is comfortable. You may be looking of more of a cognitive-behaviorally oriented therapist or what's commonly, known as CBT. This style of therapy is the most researched due to its inherent "testability". In other words, CBT interventions are didactic (instructive) in nature, and as such, fit well into formal research studies. In fact, expressive writing is considered to be in the cognitive-behavioral family of therapeutic interventions.

Most therapists tend not to exclusively identify with one therapeutic modality, but instead call themselves "eclectic". Which simply means they utilize skills and interventions from a broad range of theoretical disciplines. Each school of thought puts forth a theory sating "X" is the cause of emotional distress and therefore "Y" should be the intervention and "Z" the result (which is ideally the successful resolution to emotional problems). However, if you were to take a step back and look at the common factors among all treatment modalities a few essential components emerge. Therapeutic rapport, the counselor's empathy, and the patient's disclosure of troubling thoughts and emotions during the session. Some studies suggest the most important factor is the "accurate empathy" of the counselor. However, if you take a further step back, logically speaking, nothing in the therapy session can happen if the patient does not disclose, express, and process their inner most thoughts. This disclosure is the very essence of expressive writing. In this case you disclose to the journal and not a person.

When such disclosures do occur in therapy the therapist will encourage the free and unencumbered expression of thoughts, beliefs and emotions and values and process such content into finding meaning and insight. While expressive writing gives the writer an opportunity to make such disclosures without anyone hearing or reading it. Expressive writing offers the writer complete and total privacy. In the therapist's office, you have an audience of one. With expressive writing, your audience is yourself. In fact, the research on expressive writing shows people report the greatest benefit when they are instructed not to share their writing with anyone. They feel freer with their writing and are less likely to "hold back" or "sugarcoat" their entries, for fear of making themselves look a certain way to the one who reads the journal.

Although there is considerable overlap between making disclosures to a therapist or to a writing journal, sadly the journal cannot talk back (If it does, go see a therapist!). What a therapist can do that a journal can't is provide guidance and objective feedback. They tend to focus on the presenting problem such as depressed moods and other factors that contribute and maintain the depressed outlook. They help you create a change in your perception or interpretation of events, which can be of enormous value. A good therapist will get to know you well enough to know when it's time to call in your support network or otherwise advance you to a higher level of care, such as a hospital or other program with more supports. Ultimately it is up to you and how you are functioning in your life. If the depression/anxiety/frustration is so severe that you are contemplating suicide. Seek help immediately! On the other hand, if your symptoms have contributed to missed days at work, and is putting your job or significant relationships in jeopardy, still, it may be helpful to seek out a therapist. However, for mild preoccupation, distraction, and mood that for the most part is normative for the situation, you'd likely be fine with journaling alone. Again, this is a subjective line and only you can make that determination for yourself. My opinion is that, "when in doubt, seek 'em out". If you're on the fence of whether or not to see a counselor, go. Your therapist might even suggest expressive writing as a part of the treatment!

How Do I "Do" Expressive Writing?

Although there is no standard rule to expressive writing, most of the research suggests the maximum benefit with expressive writing comes from three to four writing sessions for about 15 to 20 minutes each. These sessions are typically guided by one or more specific writing prompts. The style of these prompts can vary from sentence completion to open-ended questions, using a picture for inspiration, or beginning a letter… etc. The idea is to help you explore significant material to you, process that content, and hopefully gain some insight and find some meaning and a measure of peace in the chaos.

You may be tempted to write for hours and hours, and if the mood strikes you, its ok to follow it. However, it is recommended not to force yourself to write for any artificial length of time. Rather, it's more helpful to engage with your writing assignments when you can mentally and emotionally focus on the topic. Your engagement with this process depends on you. To know when you're ready to explore hard felt feelings and process through tough events is at its core a subjective appraisal. Typically, in trauma treatment the concept of SUDs, or "subjective units of distress" is explained. The patient will use the SUDs scales to monitor themselves as they tell their story. On a scale of 1 to 10, where 1 is as calm as you can be and 10 is the worst distress imaginable. The ideal "SUD" to be at is between a 4 and 7. Anything less than a 4 you're not really connecting with what you're writing... you might as well be writing a grocery list. Anything higher than a 7 and you're over connecting and likely so emotionally disturbed you can't think straight, you may be physically shaking, crying, or otherwise too upset to continue the exercise. In other words, you're looking for the "goldilocks zone" of emotional distress. You want to be bothered enough to care and engage with the exercise but not too bothered that you fall apart and cannot complete the writing session.

As mentioned above, according to the research, the greatest benefit with expressive writing is found with three to four sessions for about 15 to 20 minutes each for a single traumatic event. This book provides far more than three to four writing sessions. I have included many expressive writing prompts (part 2) along with a free writing section without prompts (part 3) due to the ongoing nature of being a targeted parent. Parental alienation is not a single event, and in all likely hood, this is a fight that will be on going and take a significant amount of time. You may find it helpful to revisit the writing prompts/free writing section for a number of years to come.

My intention is to provide you, the alienated parent, with an outlet to process the stress of fighting for a connection with your kids and bolster your resiliency when your "gas tank" is running on empty. This is your book and there is no wrong way to do an expressive writing assignment, as long as you adhere to a few simple rules:

1. You must connect with your writing. Keep those SUDs in the range that's going to be most effective. As mentioned above that range would be somewhere between 4 and 7 on a 10-point scale.

2. Forget about spelling, grammar, editing... etc. simply put, this is your journal it's not for anyone to read so as long as you know what it says that's all that matters.

3. <u>By the nature of the exercise, keep the writing personal.</u> Sometimes it can help to provide context in your journal to jog your memory or help get you focused. However, too much background can distract you from expressive writing and lead you into ordinary journaling. If you notice your SUDs going down to a 2 or a 3, this can be a clue you need to refocus your topic.

4. <u>Its ok to stray from the assigned topic, if that's where your writing takes you.</u> While it is ideal to stick to the topic at hand and "dig" for connections and process your feelings. Don't be too strict when it comes to keeping on point. If while in your writing session you diverge into a side topic, that's ok. Just make sure it's still personal to you and it doesn't turn in to a grocery list!

5. <u>Don't share your writing.</u> By making a commitment to yourself that you will not share what you put down in this book you will feel free to explore those deep secrets that are only for you. If you are concerned that someone is likely to find this book and read what you write, consider ways to enforce your privacy. If it comes to it you can always tear out pages and shred them. If you do want to share some of what you've written, you can verbally tell a trusted person, so that you can "edit" in real time the things that may be a little too personal. If you feel what you have written would make a great letter to someone. Treat the exercise as a draft and re-write the letter.

6. <u>Expect your emotions to intensify.</u> At least at first. May be for an hour maybe for a day or two. Usually when you first start digging in to the emotional recesses of your mind it can bring up frustrations, fears, anxieties, and feelings of depression. These emotional spikes will usually subside in a short time, but if they persist or get acutely intense, reach out to your support network (friends/family) or consider calling a therapist.

7. <u>Above all else know when to call it quits.</u> This may seem counter intuitive, one of the rules is to stop writing. Some call it the "flip out rule". If you feel like you're going to flip out if you keep writing, remind yourself you are allowed to stop at any time.

Hostile-Aggressive Parenting (HAP)

& Parental Alienation (PA)

This section will review some basic information of what parental alienation is and what it isn't. As well as take a look at the behaviors and actions of the adults that could lead to parental alienation syndrome in the children.

What Is Hostile-Aggressive Parenting (HAP)?

Hostile-aggressive parenting is a term that describes a general pattern of behavior by a parent or guardian that induces psychological and emotional disruption, either directly or indirectly, of family relationships through manipulation, aggression, vindictiveness, and possessiveness of the children usually within the context of a divorce or post-divorce co-parenting. These behaviors, usually by the custodial parent towards the non-resident parent, seek to minimize the influence and/or parental role of the non-resident parent in an attempt to "win" litigation or otherwise maintain power or control over the other parent. This pattern of behavior is not so different from bullying insofar as the perpetrating parent is exploiting a differential of power in the post-divorce relationship. For example, since the kids spend the majority of time with the custodial parent, they are exposed to that parent's version of events and often persuaded to "join their side". In such cases, the children are engulfed in this conflict and become causalities to the war between parents. Although HAP is destructive it does not necessarily lead to parental alienation in all cases.

Signs of this hostile-aggressive parenting dynamic are anything that could interfere with the parenting time and relationship of the other parent. Such as one parent scheduling activities or events on the other parent's time. Disparaging the other parent's residence, parenting practices, choice of new partner, friends and/or family to the children. Any involvement of the children in court actions with a few exceptions. It certainly is fine and healthy to address the children's concerns about the divorce or any interparental conflict if they already know about it. However, this must be done with extreme caution to avoid any biasing weather intentional or unintentional. If concerns need to be addressed it is best to address the children's concerns together, as a united front. If that is not a possibility, explore the option of using a neutral third party such as a family counselor. In any event both parents should approach conflict from a position of love for their children not contempt for each other. Some common behaviors of a hostile-aggressive parent include:

- Refusing access to children on the designated parenting time.
- Rigid enforcement of visitation schedule (little to no cooperative flexibility).
- Admonishments or punishments to the non-resident parent for minor infractions of the parenting agreement (ex. Being 5 minutes late returning the children).
- Refusing access to schools, doctors, counselors etc.
- Arguing in front of children and "airing dirty laundry".
- Making the non-resident's parenting time ("visitation") conditional on child support payments.
- Refusing to let the child bring a special toy over to the other parent's house.
- False and inflammatory accusations that the other parent is unsafe.
- Attempting to undermine the non-resident parent's parenting time with special events (i.e. "I got tickets to the circus, but we'll have to cancel your visitation with Dad")
- Openly criticizing the non-resident parent to the children or in an area the children can hear the conversation.
- Changing the child's surname when the alienating parent remarries (creates psychological and emotional distance)
- Coaching/coercing the children to disparage the other parent to third parties (teachers, counselors, judges... etc.)
- Prompting the children to give personal details about the other parent's personal life.

- Insinuating to the children they are not safe when in the care of the non-resident parent.

What Is Parental Alienation?

Parental Alienation (PA) or Parental Alienation Syndrome (PAS) is the result of hostile-aggressive parenting when the tactics by one parent negatively affect the children's relationship with the other parent and precipitate what appears to be a child-initiated estrangement from the targeted parent. This concept originating with Dr. Richard Gardner in the 1980's has seen its fair share of controversy.

PA can be thought of in two perspectives. One is the legal perspective where lawyers advocate for their clients and the other is the mental health perspective where clinicians advocate for those afflicted with psychological and emotional distress. This is an important distinction to understand; from the legal perspective, the lawyer's client is the parent not the child. The lawyer has a duty to present the best argument to win the case not necessarily protect the children from complex psychological hardship. This is not to say that lawyers are uncaring individuals or heartless people they are just doing their jobs as directed by their clients - the children's parent. It is not the responsibility of a lawyer to protect a child from psychological and/or emotional harm, that is the parent's job. From a mental health perspective, it is very clear that high conflict divorce/hostile-aggressive parenting, leads to emotional and psychological harm to children. No clinician would disagree with that statement. With that said, this journal takes the mental health perspective, and is inclusive of all consequences of hostile aggressive parenting and parental alienation on the targeted parent's relationship ranging from mild to severe.

In Gardner's rendition of PA he identified eight characteristic symptoms that indicate parental alienation. These eight symptoms are:

1. A campaign of denigration

A crusade undertaken by the alienating parent to degrade the targeted parent to anyone who will listen. Friends, family, doctors, teachers, counselors, and the children themselves.

2. Weak, absurd, or otherwise frivolous rationalizations for the animosity toward the targeted parent

The child's reasons for distance/animosity are exaggerations of normative events or are otherwise unjustified in the course of daily life. (i.e., I don't want to see daddy because his car is always a mess)

3. Lack of ambivalence

The child feels certain in the way he or she perceives things. There is little to no room for other viewpoints or opinions with regard to the alienated parent.

4. The "independent-thinker" phenomenon

The child insists that these frivolous rationalizations are all his or her idea and that no one coached him or her to say anything.

5. Reflexive support of the alienating parent in the parental conflict

The alienating parent can do no wrong when it comes to dealings with the targeted parent

6. Absence of guilt over cruelty to and/or exploitation of the alienated parent

The child may feel and/or say, "they get what they deserve". This lack of remorse/guilt may be a façade displayed for the benefit of the alienating parent or genuinely felt by the child within a context of distorted thinking due to the indoctrination of the alienating parent.

7. The presence of borrowed scenarios

This is evident when the child and the alienating parent often use the similar or the same words of criticism or disparagement.

8. Spread of animosity to the friends and/or extended family of the alienated parent.

The child may begin to see the targeted parent's extended family as the "them" in an "us vs. them" dynamic.

These symptoms are what Dr. Gardner laid out as he described what he saw over and over again in his practice over a number of years. The clinical presentation of PA is so counterintuitive (especially with the "independent thinker" phenomenon) that many mental health clinicians miss it completely, and as a result, they too become biased against the targeted parent. This is not because they are contemptable people, they are just not trained to manage the complex presentation of parental alienation. Mental health clinicians are trained listeners, so that's what they do, they listen to their clients. Considering this, it would be essential for any clinician to get an accurate history from both parents not just one.

There is no standard metric or official diagnostic classification of PAS. Although, it can be considered that if enough of these symptoms are present to significant degree it can be indicative of Parental Alienation Syndrome. Every case of alienation is different and not every case will have all 8 characteristics present, some will vary in number and intensity to some degree. However, the end result, the dissolution of the parent-child relationship through a pattern of high conflict parenting, is the chief characteristic. The level to which PA and PAS can be conceptualized is broken up in to three categories; mild, moderate, and severe.

In some cases, the estrangement is slight, may never manifest in the child and may only represent itself in a brief hesitancy to go with the non-resident parent during the prescribed parenting time. There may be occasional "rescheduling of visitation" However, in these mild cases the bond is still strong with the targeted parent. The child will apricate the time once they are together with the that parent. Occasionally the child may go along with criticism of the alienating parent, although not usually in the presence of the targeted parent. This child is aware of the "two sides" but not actively recruited to one or another. In many cases the alienating parent is unaware of how his/her actions are contributing to the child's feelings about the other parent and is usually, but not always, willing to attempt strategies to help his/her child cope in a healthy way. The major consequence of these mild PAS cases is the diminished bond the child could have with the non-resident parent. This level of interfamilial conflict may cause some disruptions in study habits and negatively affect school performance, social relationships, self-esteem, and may contribute to manifestations of anxiety and depression.

In moderate cases, the child actively resists the prearranged parenting time attending few such visits over the course of a prolonged period. These children may openly criticize and disparage the other parent to teachers, counselors, doctors, and to the targeted parent directly. In these moderate cases the child begins to adopt distorted views of their custodial parent against their non-resident parent. These cognitive distortions are reinforced by the alienating parent and the cycle of PAS takes hold. During times when the child is with the targeted parent the child exhibits behavioral disruptions, casual disregard for the parent and usually extended family connected to the targeted parent. In some cases, the alienating parent is unaware of how their actions contribute to the significant dissolution of the non-resident parent's relationship with the child but does receive some satisfaction (rarely admitted) that the relationship is disrupted. This type of alienation can be thought of as a natural result of poor boundaries and open hostility/interference towards the non-resident parent. The major consequence of moderate alienation is the dissolution of the relationship between the non-resident parent and the child. The child could suffer academic motivation problems, general behavioral disruptions at home and school as well as out in the community. If the child is mid to late adolescence he or she may be at risk for drug experimentation, inappropriate sexualized behavior, truancy, aggression and fighting, bullying, minor to major infractions of breaking the law. Children in this category are more likely than the mild category to experience poor self-esteem, depression and/or anxiety as well as some age regressive behaviors (such as thumb sucking for younger children), gastro-intentional issues (bedwetting & soiling), psychosomatic issues (headaches), etc.

In the severe cases, the child strongly resists any contact with the targeted parent. Younger children may run to a hiding spot, where adolescent children may run out of the house. They maintain a firmly held fixed false belief that the targeted parent is bad, dangerous, or abusive. The child is likely to have a pathologically enmeshed relationship (child has diminished sense of autonomous self, but is an extension of the alienating parent) with the alienating parent. The child may make false reports of abuse, with active coaching by the alienating parent or independently in an attempt to win approval of the alienating parent. The child may or may not believe such reports of abuse, in other words sometimes the brainwashing is severe enough where the child will believe abuse happened when it never did. The alienating parent is most often aware of their contributions to the destruction of the relationship between the child and the non-resident parent. Their goal is to get rid of the other parent or "get even" with them by taking their kids away, permanently. Such efforts of the alienating parent often come at a steep psychological and emotional cost to the children. They can feel they were actually abused and suffer real psychological symptoms of PTSD as if the abuse or trauma had actually happened. Similar to the consequences of moderate alienation, severely alienated children may present with major behavioral disturbances, low school functioning, poor social functioning, self-esteem issues, depression and/or anxiety as well as there may be some age regressive behaviors (such as thumb sucking for younger children), gastro-intentional issues (bedwetting & soiling), psychosomatic issues (headaches), etc. to a more severe degree than fond in the moderately alienated category. Mid to late adolescence children are at high risk for drug use, inappropriate sexualized behavior, truancy, aggression and fighting, bullying, minor to major infractions of breaking the law.

This is not to say that all estrangement is a case of parental alienation. There are valid reasons where a child would naturally distance themselves from a parent. In some cases of actual abuse/neglect the child should be protected from the abusing parent. Other instances include a parent struggling with an active addiction to drugs or alcohol. Active mental illness is another valid reason that a child may naturally pull away from a parent. However, simply having ongoing challenges with mild to moderate mental health issues does not automatically equate to a parent being justifiably estranged from their child. In order to be diagnosed with a mental illness the symptoms must precipitate a functional impairment in an important area of the person's life. For example, someone could experience mild to moderate recurrent depression and be an adequately functioning parent as long as they are meeting the child's social, emotional, physical and educational needs. The area of impairment could be that individual's life satisfaction and not impact the performance parental responsibilities. On the other hand, if the depression is so severe that the individual cannot get out of bed to care for the children, in all likelihood, this would fall under neglect and not the result of parental alienation. Outside of these conditions, (abuse/neglect, addiction, severe mental illness), it is extremely rare that a child wants to completely cut ties with an emotionally available, normative parent.

On the following page is a brief table outlining examples of hostile-aggressive behaviors which line up with post-alienation behaviors. A before and after comparison of alienating behaviors. In the blank space below write in any behaviors you've noticed your ex do that may reflect either HAP or PA. It's important to identify specific behaviors in order to begin to recognize them for what they are, and most importantly, recognize that PA is (with the exception noted above) not your fault.

Comparative chart of typical HAP behaviors to pre/post alienation

Pre-alienation HAP behaviors	Post Alienation HAP behaviors
Actively interferes with the non-resident's parenting time (access refusal)	Claims to be "respecting child's wishes" not see other parent when the child refuses to go
Openly reluctant to comply with shared parenting and /or rigid adherence to plan when inconvenient to non-resident parent	Outright refusals claiming children do not want non-resident involvement, claiming "can't or won't force them to comply"
Degrades other parent to 3rd parties and refuses to allow access to records (doctors, teachers, lawyers… etc)	Does not inform other parent of important events concerning the child claiming they are "respecting the child's wishes"
Disparages the parent to the child or in conversations with others around children	Supports and reinforces child's distorted view of the non-resident parent
Coaches or coerces the children to disparage the other parent to third parties (teachers, counselors, judges… etc.)	Rewards the child with positive attention and/or gifts when the alienating parent's views are adopted

Unintentional brainwashing -persistent questioning of imagined abuse by the other parent	Reinforcement of the mistaken notion that the other parent is unfit/dangerous
Intentional brainwashing – persistent questioning with leading statements in an attempt to convince the children they were abused in some way by the other parent	Continues to reinforce the alienation narrative, with the intent to maintain the estrangement

The Emotional Cost Of Alienation

While there are many books about PA and how to fight against it, this book is about you and your ability to process the continuing stress of an estranged parenting relationship with your child/children. You may ask, why go through all that processing and rehashing of past and current events? What is the point of journaling such an ordeal, and where's the value?

Those are all fair questions. The simple answer is, that in order to successfully adapt to ongoing stressors in everyday life you must be free from the overbearing emotional weight of alienation. For example, if you are overly preoccupied with thinking of this situation you may forget an essential aspect of your job, that may be putting your financial security at risk. Also, the toxic emotions of unresolved grief and trauma can seep out in to your everyday relationships in the form of snapping at your significant other, driving aggressively on the road, or being dismissive and short with your family or friends. Perhaps the most severe of all, by not processing your emotional distress you could internalize those toxic emotions and begin to see only the negative in life. This is what cognitive theorists call "cognitive bias" and is one path that could lead to significant clinical depression.

Clinical depression can leave the afflicted bedridden for days, gain large amount of weight by a never-ending bingeing urge, or alternatively, lose weight by simply being too depressed to eat. The negative thinking can spiral out of control and you could end up seeing no point to life anymore. This distorted thinking can lead to having no hope for the future and thereby serious thoughts of suicide.

If you have ever thought of hurting yourself take a moment right now and program the National Suicide Prevention Lifeline into your cell phone or write it down and keep it in a safe place where you will have easy access to it. If you have had suicidal thoughts I urge you to enroll in therapy with a qualified therapist. This expressive writing guide alone is not sufficient to meet your needs.

Below are the numbers for some national helplines. These resources can be anonymous and are of enormous value when you are in distress and need to talk to someone right then and there. Helplines can be a wonderful way to get reassurance or resources when it is needed the most. Remember, if in doubt - reach out!

National Parent Helpline
1-855- 4A PARENT
(1-855-427-2736)

National Suicide
Prevention Lifeline 1-800-273-8255

Child Help USA
National Child Abuse Hotline
(800) 422-4453

SAMHSA's National
Helpline
1-800-662-HELP (4357)

Information on family legal issues and referrals
1-844-USA-GOV1
https://www.usa.gov/family-legal

Stress

Stress is one of those things that is hard to define but everybody knows what it is. Most agree that stress is a negative state of feeling that leads to the activation of the fight-flight response in reaction to the perceived importance of an event. Some stress is ok, in fact some stress is healthy. Problems arise when there's too much stress for too long. The Yerkens-Dodson law of stress and performance states that performance increases with stress, but to a point then it decreases. Simply put, you have to care enough to be motivated but not too much that you freeze up (not to dissimilar from the concept of SUDs in the preceding section). Therefor the goal is to manage stress in a healthy and balanced way not eliminate it completely.

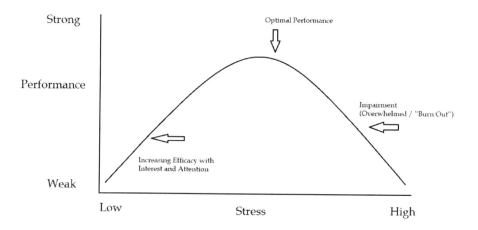

It is unrealistic to think we can get rid of all sources of stress in our lives but there are ways we can increase our resiliency, or the ability to bounce back, when stress becomes too much and starts taking its toll. Generally, in stress management the first thing to do is to identify triggers that lead to acute exacerbations of stress. Write them down and become well familiar with what happens right before you start to feel overwhelmed and look at what you do to cope with that feeling. Sometimes, your efforts to cope can actually reinforce the stress and turn a single episode into a cycle of chaos in your life.

Warning Signs Of Stress

People have an enormous capacity for self-denial. While some people stuff all their stress deep down inside themselves (leading to an eventual eruption) others seem to develop a hair trigger sensitivity to stress. In both cases the likely culprit is the accumulation of stress and not any one instance. The preverbal straw that breaks the camel's back as it were. You may think the only stress that really counts are the major events such as job loss, divorce, serious illness. This is not necessarily true. Small stressors can accumulate over time if you don't manage it. These small stressors could be something so ordinary you may not even acknowledge it as a problem. For example:

- Losing you keys, wallet, remote... etc - regularly
- Being surrounded by nosy traffic/office/home with little to no escape
- Getting less than optimal sleep
- Ongoing financial pressure
- Etc...

Recognizing the signs and symptoms that the stress is getting to you is a vitally important step towards successful stress management. Some of these can be subtle while others are rather obvious. You can recognize stress in three areas; physical, psychological and behavioral. Below are just some of the typical signs of stress you may recognize:

Physical signs of stress:

- Faster breathing
- Heart rate increasing
- Fatigue
- Muscle aches
- Dry mouth

Psychological signs of stress:

- Agitation/Hostility
- Impaired concentration
- Increased mood instability
- Feeling overwhelmed
- Intrusive or racing thoughts

Behavioral signs of stress:

- Sharp jerky movements
- Tensing muscle groups (arms, fists, jaw... etc)
- Lashing out at others (verbally/physically)
- Aggressive driving
- Missed days at work or school

If you notice yourself having any of these common signs of stress let the recognition of such be a reminder to you that you need to manage your stress rather than to react to it. The next section will review (very briefly) some tips to manage stress.

Proactive And Reactive Stress Management

There are two ways to manage your stress, proactive and reactive. Proactive strategies are the hardest to implement and follow through with due to the lack of a noticeable and immediate effect. By their very nature, if done well you will not notice its effectiveness because you are largely preventing the majority of your stress. Conversely the reactive stress management techniques have the most demonstrable effect. Actively managing your stress will require some intermixing of the two strategies. Your stress management plan will be delicate balance between the two methods that you find works best for you. Everybody is different in how they handle stress and how they cope with adversity. Here are some stress management tips:

Proactive stress management strategies:

- Start with a good night sleep
- Drink with plenty of water throughout the day
- Adopt a healthy diet
- maintain regular exercise
- Practice positive thinking
- Focus on solutions rather than problems
- Utilize your support network of family and friends

Reactive stress management strategies:

- Deep slow breathing – when acutely stressed
- Taking a break from stressful situations (if safe to do so)
- Going for a walk
- Talking to a friend or family member (about the stressor)
- Active problem solving, focusing on taking steps towards a solution
- Challenging negative thoughts and coping practices (don't automatically assume the worst)
- Utilize expressive journaling

By adopting some of these proactive and reactive stress management strategies into your daily routine you can lower your overall stress levels. There will always be stress in your life, it us unrealistic to think we can ever "get rid of" our stress. However, by becoming aware of our stress warning signs we can make a meaningful impact on how we experience stress and increase our efficacy in managing the challenges in life.

Part 2 – Prompted writing assignments

Writing Prompts

For the most benefit from these exercises it is recommended that you engage with the writing assignments with in a designated time frame, that you set. Depending on the content of your writing subject (i.e. a specific incident or an ongoing ordeal) you may want to set an initial goal of at least three days but no more than two weeks for a single event. There will be opportunity for you to continue your journaling daily if you like in the next part of this book, the unstructured writing section.

Through the structured section each assignment will start with a prompt followed by 4 pages (with the exception of the first prompt having 8 pages). Don't worry if you don't fill up all 4 pages this writing is for you to process your trauma of being separated from your child, if you express what you need to express in 2 or 3 that's fine. If you feel you are going to run over, consider adding some loose-leaf pages to the relevant sections. This is your journal to do with as you please. If you think it would be helpful use photographs, sketches, old crayon artwork that use to be on the refrigerator. Use anything that will help you connect and unblock painful memories while you process through them. The goal is to be able to spend time with the memories with a decreased amount of pain and sorrow so that you can be more effective with your goals and healthy functioning in life.

Today is _____, it is the start of my writing journal. I will write for _____ minutes every _____ (frequency) for _____ (duration). I will remember to "let go" and "dig deep" for my deepest emotions and thoughts. I won't be afraid to feel them. If I feel them too intensely I can take a break, if I'm not connecting enough I will come back to it when I'm ready. I will tell myself its ok to cry, I will keep writing. I will tell myself its ok to miss my child, I will keep writing. I will tell myself its ok to grieve the relationship that has been lost so that I can move forward with my life. I will process through these feelings and emotions of loss and grief and not be ruled by them. This is my story, this is what is going on:

_____

_____

_____

_____

_____

_____

_____

_____

_____

_____

_____

_____

_____

_____

_____

_____

_____

_____

_____

_____

What happened that led to the separation? This is not about blame, either for yourself or your ex. This is about understanding your past so you can manage your future. Look for patterns in your past, reflect on types of relationships you engage in, be honest with yourself and "dig deep".

_____

_____

_____

_____

_____

_____

_____

_____

_____

_____

_____

_____

_____

_____

_____

_____

_____

_____

_____

How has your relationship changed with your child? You may be tempted to avoid "digging deep" here. Remember to keep your SUD level between a 4 and 7 on a 10- point scale (for a refresher of SUDs see pg 17).

_____

_____

_____

_____

_____

_____

_____

_____

_____

_____

_____

_____

_____

_____

_____

_____

_____

_____

_____

_____

_____

_____

What specifically has your ex done to contribute to the estrangement of your relationship between you and your child(ren). Use dates and times if helpful. Additionally, if you could tell your ex how you feel what would you say?

_____

_____

_____

_____

_____

_____

_____

_____

_____

_____

_____

_____

_____

_____

_____

_____

_____

_____

_____

Find a picture of a special day with your child, describe the day. Where was this picture taken, what happened on that day? Don't for to "dig deep" and keep your SUD level between 4-7 on a 10-point scale.

_____

_____

_____

_____

_____

_____

_____

_____

_____

_____

_____

_____

_____

_____

_____

_____

_____

_____

_____

_____

Describe a regret. This is where you "dig deep" and practice honest self-reflection, not self-blame or punishment. The goal is to acknowledge your flaws and highlight areas to improve yourself.

Describe a cherished memory. After the hard work of the previous writing assignment, this assignment should be an enjoyable trip down memory lane. It may end up being bittersweet, it may highlight the ever-present estrangement. However, it is not healthy to avoid thinking of cherished memories. It is healthy to reflect and reminisce with tears of sorrow and joy.

_____

_____

_____

_____

_____

_____

_____

_____

_____

_____

_____

_____

_____

_____

_____

_____

_____

_____

If you could talk to your child, or talk freely, what would you say?

_____

_____

_____

_____

_____

_____

_____

_____

_____

_____

_____

_____

_____

_____

_____

_____

_____

_____

_____

_____

_____

_____

_____

What are you doing for yourself? How are you keeping yourself healthy? How are you taking your power back? Describe your self-care activities, if none exist, write a plan how to incorporate them into your schedule. You need to make time for yourself. Review the stress management section if needed.

Describe another cherished memory. Same as above, do not shy away from connecting emotionally with the memory. It's ok to miss and long for the day. It is ok to miss and long for how the relationship use to be. Spend time with these cherished memories they are a part of your life.

_____

_____

_____

_____

_____

_____

_____

_____

_____

_____

_____

_____

_____

_____

_____

_____

_____

_____

_____

_____

What are your goals? (personal/parental/career/relationships). Frame your goals as SMART goals: S- specific, M- measurable, A- achievable, R-relevant, T- Time frame. For example, instead of saying "to get my son back" consider rephrasing as, "I will file with the court a complaint/modification for increased visitation time from 1 day a week to 3. I will file on Friday of this week". If you're interested in learning more about SMART goals, a very common goal setting strategy, I highly recommend learning more about the topic. However, for the purpose of expressive writing any goal format you like will be fine.

_____

_____

_____

_____

_____

_____

_____

_____

_____

_____

_____

_____

_____

_____

_____

_____

_____

_____

_____

_____

What are you most afraid of related to your estrangement? In order to get over your fear you must face it head on. Challenge yourself to rationalize your fear. A good way to do this, is after you've identified your greatest fear, imagine what you would say to a friend if they had said this as their greatest fear. You can write this assignment as a dialogue between friends, as a narrative, or journal entry. This is your journal, there is no wrong way to use it.

_____

_____

_____

_____

_____

_____

_____

_____

_____

_____

_____

_____

_____

_____

_____

_____

_____

_____

_____

_____

_____

Describe another cherished memory. After facing your fears give yourself a reward and relive a special day with your child or children. As with before, don't shy away from or otherwise avoid feeling your feelings through this process. It's is ok to cry. It is ok to mourn the past. Expressing the feelings here will help you manage your feelings in day to day life.

_____

_____

_____

_____

_____

_____

_____

_____

_____

_____

_____

_____

_____

_____

_____

_____

_____

_____

_____

_____

_____

Write a letter to your son/daughter that will <u>not</u> be sent. Looking back at the previous writing prompt asking "what would you say to your child", how would you put that message in to a letter that is age/developmentally appropriate for your child to read or hear. This assignment specifies the letter <u>not</u> be sent because this journal is what you "want" to say. After this exercise you may want to consider rewriting this letter to one that you may consider sending. Keep in mind, however, in all likelihood the letter will be intercepted by the alienating parent or alternatively freely given to them by your child. If your child is in therapy and you have an open dialogue with his or her therapist, you may consider asking if he or she is willing to read your letter in session with your child.

_____

_____

_____

_____

_____

_____

_____

_____

_____

_____

_____

_____

_____

_____

_____

_____

_____

_____

What are you going to do now? What do you want to accomplish in the next 5 years? Incorporate your goals from the previous section and describe in detail how you plan to achieve them. The goal of this book is to help you manage your emotional distress so that you can maintain or increase you functioning in life and as a parent. This is where you create a written plan of action for your future, however you envision it.

Part 3 – Free Writing

Made in the USA
Middletown, DE
11 May 2018